UNEARTHING

US

Poems and Practices
for Discovering Our Fullest Selves

JOE DAVIS

UNEARTHING US
Poems and Practices for Discovering Our Fullest Selves

Cover and interior image: digital illustration by Kristin Miller, with textures from petekarici, olegagafonov, oxygen, simonidajordjevic, via Getty Images, and paper texture from Company Folders, Inc.
Cover and interior design: Kristin Miller
Interior typesetting: Josh Eller
Editor: Dawn Rundman
Project Manager: Julie O'Brien

ISBN: 978-1-5064-9999-4
Manufactured in USA

28 27 26 25 24   1 2 3 4 5 6 7 8 9 10

This book is dedicated to all those discovering who they are. May you dig deep and unearth more than you ever imagined possible.

To the Reader

Although I don't have a green thumb, I've always loved gardens.

From hearing the sacred stories of Eden and Gethsemane, going to summer camp at the International Peace Gardens as a child, and watching the way my mom cared for the irises, daylilies, marigolds, and zinnias blossoming in front of our home every spring—some of my most impactful life lessons were found growing in gardens.

Among my favorite garden memories is my time spent planting pineapples in Jamaica. In an effort to dig deeper into the roots of my family tree, I drove across the island to learn more about the rich history and culture of the country in which my mother was born.

During my stay at a cozy cottage in the mountains of Maroon Town, an elderly groundskeeper named Jafud welcomed me with an armful of freshly plucked star fruit. We quickly became friends, talking for hours while sitting on the edge of an old moss-covered bathtub in the backyard. To his surprise, I even joined him in the daily task of tending to the half dozen acres of pineapples, yams, and star fruit that stretched into a vast rainforest beyond the bungalow.

As we sweat under the sweltering Caribbean sun, cutting away excessive shrubs and carving holes to make space for more planting, Jafud told me stories from years of working with the land. Wandering through the nearby caves and hills from the time he was a youth, he gained a simple yet profound wisdom. He knew that to walk with nature is to walk with the divine.

With swift yet gentle jabs, he turned his machete into a shovel, loosening the hardened surface to reveal the soft soil below.

Deeper.

He expressed gratitude for life's providence and how the Almighty has given us everything we could ever need.

Deeper.

We've been blessed with a fertile earth endlessly yielding vegetables, fruits, and herbs for our bodies' well-being; a sun sustaining light, heat, and warmth for our vitality; trillions of trees providing shelter and cleansing the air of pollutants; and hundreds of rivers and streams generously flowing with life.

Deeper.

With an awe-inspired twinkle in his eyes, he exclaimed how we're all intricately and inextricably connected to this boundless ecosystem of abundance.

Deeper still.

After some digging and some chopping, he pulled up the biggest pineapple I've ever seen, brushed off a few clods of dirt, and handed it to me.

That's when it dawned on me:

We are not only gardeners of the soil,
we are gardeners of the *soul*.

We are the garden.

When we tend to each other, we grow.

And the more we grow, the more we come to know who we are is more than enough.

Buried deep down under the fallow ground of anxiety and depression or the towering dung heaps of systemic oppression, all creation pulses with the possibility of flourishing.

I know this to be true from my personal experience. As I've struggled to care for my own mental, emotional, and spiritual health while navigating our collective grief and trauma, it's been the communal healing wisdom gathered in the poems and practices offered in these pages that has guided me closer to home, closer to wholeness, and, at times, even saved my life.

What you hold in your hands is not just a book of garden poems. It's a collection of metaphors for life to unearth and reclaim the best of ourselves.

Whenever I write, I'm digging deeper for the truth that's already within me and within each of us. A truth that is liberative, inclusive, and expansive. My work as an artist is the communal cultivation of abundance. I hope you join me in this ongoing process of unearthing our truest, most authentic selves. Whether or not you identify as a gardener or an artist, there's always room to grow more joy and beauty within us and around us.

Here's to our well-being.
Here's to our flourishing.
Here's to our abundance!

CONTENTS

Flourish
Poems for cultivating abundance

PLANT

Poems for planting seeds

Sing to All You Plant

Sing to all you plant,
sing to all you plant,
to honor the garden
where all life began,
sing to all you plant.

Sing to all you plant,
sing to all you plant,
to honor the people,
to honor the land,
sing to all you plant.

Imagine God singing
all life into being,
soundwaves into light,
music and meaning,
orchestral orchards,
heartbeats and heartstrings,
each chorus transforming
our thoughts into things

Imagine us singing
in harmony,
parts of you ringing
with parts of me,
a spark in you
matches a spark in me
and we're sparkling
'til the dark starts to sing
a light in my heart
when it's hard to see,
a breath of fresh air
when it's hard to breathe
an a cappella artistry

like gardeners singing
while gardening

If singing to your plants
can help new leaves grow,
imagine what singing
can do for people

Can we sing ourselves
back from the distance?
Can we sing ourselves
back to remembrance?

Sing being human
back to human beings?
Sing unity back to communities?

If there is life or death within our tongues
which do we choose to plant within our songs?

Whether we serenade or chant,
whisper or hum,
may our songs be as beautiful
as we wish to become.

Sing to all you plant,
sing to all you plant,
to honor the garden
where all life began,
sing to all you plant.

Sing to all you plant,
sing to all you plant,
to honor the people,
to honor the land,
sing to all you plant.

An Unearthing Practice

After a day spent repairing a busted tire from driving
through the mountains of Jamaica, I was exhausted and
ready to collapse on the floor. But the live reggae music
spilling into the streets from a nearby jam band lifted
my spirit.

Whenever I'm struggling with thoughts and feelings of
insecurity and self-doubt, singing and dancing to my
favorite songs help me remember the truth of who I am
and what's possible.

There are many cultures that sing as an act of healing,
and we can be counted among them. I've heard stories
of communities gathering around an individual who's
committed a wrongdoing only to sing songs that
remind them of the truth of who they are and what's
possible together.

What are songs that help you remember the truth of who
you are? What songs remind you of new possibilities?

Find your signature soundtrack by creating a playlist of
those songs to sing for yourself or alongside others.

Sing as often as you can, as loudly as you can, with
as many people as you can.

If singing can help plants grow, imagine what it can
do for people!

Bless the Earth

If a flower isn't growing,
don't curse the flower–
bless the earth.

Water the roots,
soften the dirt,
tend to the wounds,
help heal the hurt.

Life grows when blessed,
not when it's cursed–
can we create the needed
environment first?

No fruit stolen by birds or wriggling worms,
no seeds choked by prisons of thistles and thorns,
no sun-parched petals withered and scorn,
no stems cut short since the day they were born,
no leaves and roots torn before fully formed–
but a refuge, a haven, a home safe from harm.

Don't blame the bloomless for droughts with no rain,
don't shame the shriveled left out in the shade,
don't guilt the wilted, instead ease their pain–
help them find shelter for when seasons change.

The rejected and abandoned become celebrated
when we see the sacred in the desecrated.
When we remove all that robs God's breath,
we all breathe more deeply in the process.

If a flower isn't growing,
don't curse the flower–
bless the earth.

Water the roots,
soften the dirt,
tend to the wounds,
help heal the hurt.

Life grows when blessed,
not when it's cursed–
can we create the needed
environment first?

If the seeds are our children
what gardens are we building?
Does the soil that surrounds us
help heal them or kill them?

If the seeds are our children
what gardens are we building?
One with sunlight and water
and proper nutrition?

Can we create the conditions
for a world without prisons
so their dreams and visions
can reach full fruition?

No handcuffs or shackles,
no chains or cages,
no miseducation
like slaves on plantations.

If the seeds are our children,
how do we raise them
in spaces of love, compassion, and patience,
replacing degradation with more graciousness?

When the soil's cultivated
we change relationships:

Nothing grows
when the soil is bad;
all life grows
when the soil is good.

We bless our children—and all those living—
when we heal the whole neighborhood.

If a child isn't growing,
don't curse the child—
bless the earth.

If at home, school,
or in the church,
tend to their wounds,
help heal their hurt.

Life grows when blessed,
not when it's cursed—
let's create the needed
environment first.

An Unearthing Practice

Whenever I visit Jamaica, a part of me feels more alive. The wide expanse of rich green rainforest stretching as far as the eye can see, the soothing sounds of ocean waves gently crashing against the shore, fresh fruits and vegetables growing in abundance—all help me see the possibility of flourishing.

No matter where I travel, I've noticed the difference in how my body feels when I'm in spaces that are cluttered and neglected compared to spaces with thriving plants or beautiful art.

The key to healthy plants is a healthy, well-resourced environment. The same can be said about us. Changing the way our environment looks and feels can alter our mood, boost our energy, and enhance our overall wellness.

List ways you can add color and vibrancy to spaces that feel dull and lifeless.

List ways you can invest in community supports and resources that help promote life-affirming spaces in your neighborhood and beyond.

Forgot: We Are Seeds

They tried to stomp us.

What they forgot was:
we're unstompable,
unconquerable,
more than conquerors
ever thought we were.

They tried to crush us.

What they forgot was:
we rise like the dust,
like dawn after dusk,
even in the dark
a light is guiding us.

The harm they sent to us
was never meant for us.
Every weapon formed against
transforms into instruments.

Like a shovel or a shear,
make way,
make it clear:

For hundreds of years
they tried to bury us
under shame and fear.

We persist, persevere, and insist:
WE'RE STILL HERE.

They tried to break us
and yet we break free
and keep breaking free
until we all are freed.

They tried to stomp us but forgot that:

we
are
seeds.

They can't keep us down,
they can't hold us back,
we blossom and bloom
what they think we lack.

We spring from the ground,
bust through every crack,
we're stronger and wiser
with every attack!

They don't know
what they throw,
like the soil,
makes us grow.
They don't know
what they throw is fuel to the fire.
They don't know
what they throw will hurl us higher.
The ashes of their empire
serve as fertilizer!

They thought then
they had us boxed in,
fallen and downtrodden,
forsaken and forgotten,
yet God was planting,
God was plotting,
plot twist:
what they put on top of us
to stop us,
did not block us but
were the blocks to prop us up
and we're still cropping up!

Sowing seeds,
so win, seeds,
so when seeds are broken,
golden green
petals, leaves,
hopes, and dreams are opened
and no force
on all the earth
could come close to ever closing them,
when every force of heaven will make sure
we keep on growing them:
testaments and testimonies from the tests,
messiahs and messengers from the mess,
our suffering lessens when we gain lessons
from our losses we lose less
and we suck seeds from the fruit of our success.

We are seeds.

An Unearthing Practice

When tracing my cultural ancestry in Jamaica, I learned about Queen Nanny of the Maroons, one of the island's most revered heroes, who fiercely fought against British colonialism to free her people from slavery. She joined Maroons and runaways to build refugee villages in the mountains where many of their cultures and traditions remain intact to this day.

Learning about the resilience of our family or community can be inspiring and empowering.

As a practice, research the history of your family or your community—those who you are related to by blood or those you have chosen or who have chosen you—and collect stories of overcoming adversity.

Find a creative way to save and share these stories with others, such as online archives, photo books, journals, or storytelling gatherings.

Can You Dig It?

I'm a truth-seeker
    'cuz I know the truth's deeper
        than what you see first on the surface

Can you dig it?

I'm a truth-seeker
    'cuz I know the truth's deeper
        than a Google or Wikipedia search

Can you dig it?

I'm a truth-seeker
    'cuz I know the truth's deeper
        than what the media
            is spoon-feedin' us by force

Can you dig it?

Gotta dig deep into the root,
    spit out the seed and eat the fruit
        until you needn't any proof
            what you seek is seeking you

Can you dig it?

If you really wanna reach
        a deeper level,
            you can't just think about it,
              you're gonna need a shovel

Can you dig it?

Truth is only as deep
    as it was buried
        underneath all the
            emotions and beliefs
                that you've carried

Can you dig it?

You gotta dig deeper
        to the truth in your soul,
            you can't lean on a shovel
                and pray for a hole

Can you dig it?

        the deeper you dig
      the closer you grow
    from a God-shaped hole
  to a God-shaped *whole*
  unearthing the truth
that you already know.

An Unearthing Practice

When working with my friend Jafud on a pineapple farm in Jamaica, I learned how to prepare the soil before planting. It was necessary to overturn layers of dirt and dig a deep enough hole for roots to take hold.

While reflecting and journaling about the cultivation process, I was reminded of times I needed to work through negative emotions and limiting beliefs before I could fully express myself. It was necessary to overturn the old layers that were no longer contributing to my growth in order for the truest parts of myself to reemerge.

Ask yourself what fears hold you back.

Ask yourself what hopes inspire you to move forward.

Sometimes these can be described as pain points and pleasure points, or triggers and glimmers. This is when we feel highly charged emotions activating triggers of stress or glimmers of hope.

Give yourself the time and space needed to sit with your fears, self-doubt, and insecurities. Welcome support from others if you can.

Write down your limiting beliefs in one column and your unlimiting beliefs in another.

Write down your weakest beliefs in one column and your strongest beliefs in another.

Think about the difference between the two columns.

Think about what it would take to close the gap between the two.

Practice doing whatever it takes to close the gap between the two.

Continue to "overturn the layers" until you get deep enough to root and connect with a true, authentic sense of self.

Dirty

When I was a child
I played in the dirt
and I laughed
and I smiled . . .

But now
I scrub away the dirt
with soap and water
and a wash towel . . .

Maybe I don't wanna be
like dirty people
in the street . . .

Maybe I don't wanna see
the dirt on my hands and feet . . .

Maybe none of us look
under the rugs . . .
we sweep

Maybe if we weren't blinded
by dust . . .
we'd weep

Have our fingers failed to feel the filth
beneath our fingernails . . .
like the deep rich soil
where the nutrients are held . . .
like darkened prison cells
where a wealth of genius dwells . . .
like seeing those excel . . .
as excrement expelled . . .

. . . what if the parts of us exed out, exiled, and forgot
are really buried treasure where x marks the spot?
. . . what if the worst place
is a hurt place
where we're told we don't deserve grace
. . . and being treated like we're unworthy
is why we wound up there in the first place?

. . . what if we don't try to hide it or deny it
but realize that for life to thrive . . .
a little dirt might be required.

Can we reach closer to the dirt
. . . to unearth our hurt?
Can we reach closer to the dirt
. . . to unearth our worth?

We are messy and imperfect
and perfectly loved because
this earth cares for us
just as a mother does.

So the next time we won't be so judgy
when someone reminds us
our own heart is dusty.

So the next time I get dirty,
I'll smile and laugh
knowing that the dirt
is always smiling back.

An Unearthing Practice

Although the Caribbean is internationally celebrated for its rich food, music, and culture, it's also stigmatized because of the impoverished conditions that come from a history of colonization.

We can often be quick to judge someone in a different life circumstance than our own without questioning what happened for them to be in that situation or considering how we might be more similar to them than we'd like to admit.

Reflect on a time when you were judged prematurely and how you would have preferred to be treated. How can this inform how we look at other people? How can this create space for more empathy and compassion?

Next time you're near dirt, touch it with your hands or feet and think about the rich nutrients it holds. Next time you're near someone struggling, connect with them and think about the wisdom and beauty they hold.

They're Rooting for Us

They've been rooting for us
since we came,
the first day we've been here.

They're rooting for us to return,
reclaim, and remember.

They're rooting for us all to rise
as high as we can,
and if we ever fall,
they'll help us rise again.

They're rooting for us
to realign with the true vine
through reunification,
for us to find a direct line
of communication.

They carry us on their shoulders,
they carry us over, carry us forward,
and everywhere they carry us
we carry their culture.

They strengthen us and lift us up,
they give as much
as they can give to us,
they give us hope,
they give us love,
they give everything,
but they don't give up.

Their generous love replenishes us,
no distance can diminish this lineage.
It's in our skin, it's in our blood,
their healing wisdom lives in us.

Though many tried to break us
as far as we can trace us,
we learn from their mistakes
and build upon their greatness.

Nothing can separate us:
from ancestors
from the most high
to the deepest depths of us

the best of us
still rest in us
breath to lungs

most benevolent
essence
of us

the body
mind
spirit
protecting us
helping us
blessing us
the best of us

the source of love
is the only force
that doesn't force us

they route the courses
through the core of us
in every chorus
a mighty fortress
the seeds before the forest

they pass the torches
so we can find them
they left the lights on
outside their porches
they're rooting with us,
within us,
and always rooting for us.

An Unearthing Practice

Marcus Garvey, one of Jamaica's national heroes, famously wrote, "A people without knowledge of their past history, origin, and culture is like a tree without roots." This is one of the reasons why I travel to my mother's birthplace and honor my elders and ancestors as often as possible.

Make a list of all the supports and resources, people and places, that helped you throughout your life.

Are there caregivers, teachers, mentors, friends, siblings? Are there youth centers, schools, churches, nonprofits, businesses, community spaces?

Reflect on how this village of love has shaped and continues to shape who you are today. Reach out and give a phone call, thank-you card, or gift to express your appreciation.

You can also study the lineage of your heroes and those you respect and admire to learn about the community of people who helped influence them.

Break Through

What happens when we break?

Do we break up, break down,
break out, or break through?

How much of us needs to break
for us to be made new?

Not just our hearts
but every part,
scattered and scarred,
shattered like shards,
they got it right
when they said it was hard.

I've never felt so close to death.
Why is this not over yet?
To get over this
I've done all I know how to do,
I close my eyes and hold my breath,
'cuz the only way out is through.

Oppressed, suppressed,
repressed, depressed,
together we press on.

When I feel broken,
you show me my whole self,
when I feel weak,
you teach me I am strong.

I only know courage
because I've known fear.
I only know hope
because I've known despair.

I've known destruction
and I've known disaster
and learned how to live
happily even after.

The sadness I have in the aftermath
was gathered as I traveled the path.

The more I let go
of avoiding the void,
the space to grieve
made more space for joy.

Oppressed, suppressed,
repressed, depressed,
together we press on.

When I feel broken,
you show me my whole self,
when I feel weak,
you teach me I am strong.

There's a healing we feel
only after the pain,
colors we see
only after the rain.

When we finally lay down
the burden of shame,
we have nothing to lose
but our chains.

What I felt was breaking me,
was really just breaking free.

Breaking toxic relationships,
breaking generational curses,
breaking despair through hope,
breaking fear through courage.

With the strength of our roots,
supports, and resources,
we can break through together
and collectively flourish.

Oppressed, suppressed,
repressed, depressed,
together we press on.

When I feel broken,
you show me my whole self,
when I feel weak,
you teach me I am strong.

How much of us needs to break
for us to be made new?

Enough to show us
we are not broken,
our whole selves
are breaking through.

Not a newer self,
but truer self,
nothing more left to say or do.

Unbecoming all that isn't us
until all that remains is true.

An Unearthing Practice

The time spent in the hot sun working on the Jamaican farm was long and hard. Although I didn't get to enjoy the fruit of my labor at the end of the day, I knew everything I harvested and ate was a result of others who had toiled long before I had even arrived–and for that I gave thanks.

Today's discipline is tomorrow's ease.

As a practice, it can build your capacity to manage stress if you do one thing that makes you uncomfortable every day.

Some practices might include engaging in physical exercise, taking a cold shower, or eating bitter or bland foods that are actually healthy for you.

These are called "controlled reps"–intentionally creating moments of discomfort. The more you engage the unpleasant sensations you experience in your body, the more you develop a relationship with them and become more tolerant, more accepting, and ultimately more capable of adapting to unexpected changes.

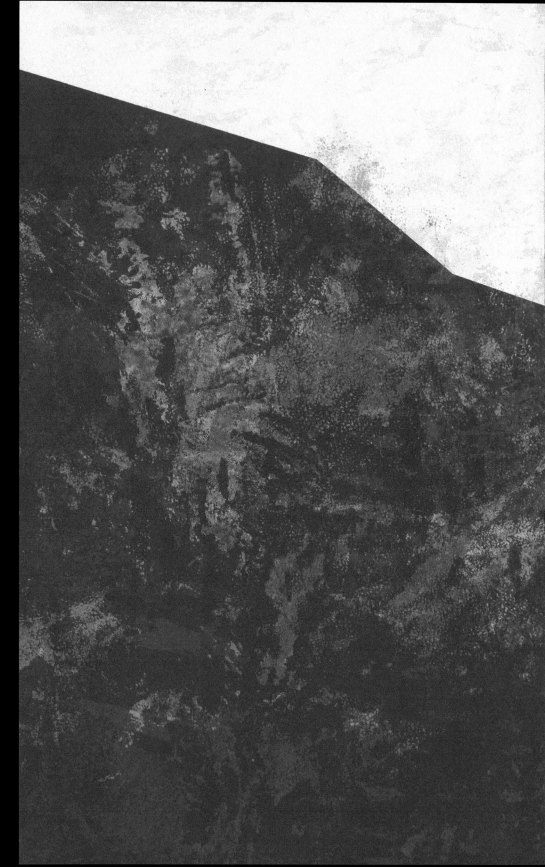

GROW

Poems for growth

Green Light

When you need the light
but can't see the light,
let this be the green light
to go *be* the light.

When ya soul says YES!
but the haters say NO!

I say let my people glow,
let my people glow!

When the world says STOP!
but ya heart says GO!

I say let my people glow,
let my people glow!

Even if you're moving slow,
even if you gotta stop,
let 'em know you got that glow
and let it shine—
no matter what

No need to ask permission,
no need to have it hidden,
do not apologize
for the magic of existence

The world is dull and dim if it's never seen
how to grow through the snow
like an evergreen,
you're unique and bring life
to each and every scene,
when there's a better you
then there's a better me

When ya soul says YES!
but the haters say NO!

I say let my people glow,
let my people glow!

When the world says STOP!
but ya heart says GO!

I say let my people glow,
let my people glow!

You got a light that makes the whole world light,
and to shine it bright is your birthright

It's too divine to be confined
in any space, at any time
by red signs or redlines,
by doubts inside your very mind.

Can't shade it,
can't fade it,
and no need to fake it,
when the image you're made in
is holy and sacred.

Your light might be the one
that shines for someone else,
giving a hope they've never seen,
a warmth they never felt.

So when the last snowflake
of the winter melts,
I pray you remember this
and you remember well:

your soul shines with an infinite wealth
and the only person you gotta convince
is yourself.

When ya soul says YES!
but the haters say NO!

I say let my people glow,
let my people glow!

When the world says STOP!
but ya heart says GO!

I say let my people glow,
let my people glow!

An Unearthing Practice

Although my mother was born and raised in Jamaica,
I often felt like I wasn't Jamaican enough when visiting
the island, and I jokingly called myself "Jamerican."
It wasn't until many natives reminded me I had as much
of a right as anyone to fully claim my ancestry, especially
as I honored the people, the land, and the culture.

Imposter syndrome happens when we feel like a fake,
fraud, or phony in spite of experiences that
prove otherwise.

There have been times when I've been given gifts,
compliments, awards, or accolades that I felt I wasn't
worthy or deserving of receiving. Thankfully, I've
learned that my value is in who I am and not dependent
on my efforts, my achievements, or what anyone else
says or thinks about me. Knowing this, I can show up
more unapologetically with authenticity and integrity,
taking the opportunity to practice letting go of the
desire for external validation.

Are there areas of your life where you feel imposter
syndrome? Name one thing you want to do that would
make you feel more authentic and more fully self-
expressed, but you've been too nervous, ashamed, or
embarrassed to do it.

Practice doing it.

Maybe at first it's only in the comfort and safety of your
own home at first; then maybe with a trusted friend;
and hopefully, after your body has gathered up enough
courage, you can do it in front of more and more
people. With each repetition, you build confidence. You
do best what you do most!

Dancing in the Dark

Can the darkness be a space
to expand and explore?

if we can bloom in the dark
then what would we fret for?

no need to wrestle,
when we can let go,
we can rest more

no need to grip with all our might,
fist so tight we make our hands sore

we can turn the war zones
and battlegrounds
into playgrounds and dance floors

find the bliss
on the other side of risk
and take a chance more

this darkness teaches us
to be at peace
to learn as the plants learn
to live into the questions,
accepting less easy answers

there's no need
for pruning or uprooting
in a season of planting
why would we choose to fight
when instead we could be dancing?

An Unearthing Practice

I've never seen the constellations shine as brightly and clearly as I have when gazing at the night sky in the mountains of Maroon Town.

We often relate nighttime or darkness to fear or uncertainty. Yet when looking at the ink black expanse overhead, I felt a sense of peace within the mystery.

Are there questions you can make peace with not knowing the answer? Write a list of those questions.

The Stretch

if i feel too small
or get stuck and stall
can i climb, can i crawl
like the vines on a wall

growing green crescendos
bending tendrils and tentacles
against fences and windowsills
until hitting a pinnacle

we have the same strength to stretch within us all:
a gentle push
a gentle pull
expand the body
and the soul

breathe. through the stretch.
breathe through. the stretch.
breath is a bridge
to reach
to the next.

breathe through the. stretch.
breathe through the stretch.
breath is a bridge
to reach
to our best.

when i become twisted, tangled, and knotted
i press into places sharpened and hardened
and i stay long enough to move beyond it,
to gather the strength that was long forgotten

we stretch
to test the breadth of our soul,
how far can we go, how much can we grow,
how much we let go, how much can we hold,
are we much more or less than what we were told?

soften the gaze
loosen the jaw
unclench the fist
open the palms

unfolding like poetry
flowing with songs
this music was inside of us all along

breathe. through the stretch.
breathe through. the stretch.
breath is a bridge
to reach
to the next.

breathe through the. stretch.
breathe through the stretch.
breath is a bridge
to reach
to our best.

like the vines i too reach
alongside those around me
reaching high as i can
beyond barriers and boundaries

the walls are only there so i can lean and rest
the deepest stretch needs the deepest breath

slowly slowly
inch by inch
grow with purpose
with intent

as my body stretches so does my faith
and i no longer fear that either will break

it's uncomfortable
and vulnerable
yet the only way i've learned to grow

one breath at a time,
one stretch at a time,
we become a little more
of ourselves
every time.

breathe. through the stretch.
breathe through. the stretch.
breath is a bridge
to reach
to the next.

breathe through the. stretch.
breathe through the stretch.
breath is a bridge
to reach
to our best.

An Unearthing Practice

I rented a car to drive through Jamaica not realizing that it would be one of the most stressful experiences of my entire life!

I wasn't accustomed to the driver's seat being on the right side of the car, all of the cars driving on the left side of the road, honking car horns as an indicator of passing, and speed limits functioning more as suggestions of minimum speed.

My nervous system was on overdrive, but slow and intentional breathing helped me get through.

As a practice, pay attention to your breath and bodily sensations when taking the following postures.

Hold your body with the posture of someone who is rich. Move around in this posture and ask how it makes you feel.

Hold your body with the posture of someone who is renowned. Move around in this posture and ask how it makes you feel.

Hold your body with the posture of someone who is powerful. Move around in this posture and ask how it makes you feel.

Is there a difference between any of these postures and how you normally hold your body?

If so, what was the difference?

If so, why was there a difference?

Channel the Charge

Like fire in my belly,
like lightning in my heart,
I can feel the anger rising
but can I channel its charge?

If I hold it in,
it can be erosive.
If I let go of it,
it can be explosive.

I can hurt myself
or whoever's closest
if it controls me
more than I control it.

Why do these emotions
feel so big and uncontrollable?
I feel overwhelmed and can't hold it all.

If I can't stop it when it overflows,
can I direct where the current goes?
Anchor a chain before the bulldoze,
release some smoke
so no volcano blows.

Like fire in my belly,
like lightning in my heart,
I can feel the anger rising
but I can channel its charge.

Not charging towards those next to me,
who are not a threat to me,
but towards the systems oppressing,
towards the ideas vexing me,
towards the same complicity
and toxicity
that rest in me.

If you and I charge together we
can start a fire big enough to set us free.
Let us burn away the cages,
burn away the bars,
with a sun fire raging and
emblazoned in our hearts.

An Unearthing Practice

When I first saw the poverty and socioeconomic injustice in Jamaica, it made me angry, and I wanted to do something about it. As much as I wish I could end the problems overnight, the most helpful and useful action I could take was to listen and learn from those impacted as they shared ways to support their collective efforts such as educating others to increase awareness and contributing to the local economy.

I've learned that whenever I feel strong emotions, it can be helpful to channel my heightened energy towards change.

What's something that makes you really angry?

Ask yourself why it makes you feel this way.

If there's nothing you can do to create outward change, is there something you can do to create inward change?

Are there others who might also be working on the same changes? Explore ways to connect and work on those changes together.

Rhythm of Life

a rhythm when you rise,
a rhythm when you sleep,
we all got rhythm if you listen to the beat.

there's a time for rest,
a time to work,
a time to bless,
a time to curse,
a time for death,
a time for birth,
a time for everything on the earth.

what goes in
must come out

what goes up
must go down

our limbs reach for the heavens
while our roots cleave to the ground

we walk in between these worlds
where many truths can be found

move at a slow speed
or at full speed,
whatever the pace
you feel your soul needs
you can hear the rhythm
if you listen to the pulse beat

Finding your rhythm
is finding your flow.
It's human.
It's nature.
And we are both.

An Unearthing Practice

On the last day of my Jamaica trip, I was disappointed to rush through heavy traffic only to arrive at the Bob Marley Museum as it was closing. However, after pleading with the gatekeeper, my friends and I were allowed to enter for just a few minutes. As "luck" would have it, it was in those brief moments that we ran into the famous reggae musician Bongo Herman, who invited me to play hand drums with him. He taught me to slow down long enough to listen to "the rhythm of life," those unexpected experiences of magic and miracles that leave us in awe.

As a practice, take time to track and write down your patterns for a day. A pattern can be anything you did repeatedly or routinely, often without giving it much thought.

What are patterns you want to continue? What are patterns you no longer want to continue?

Consider how even your unwanted patterns might have been needed at some point and allow yourself to release them with grace.

What's a new pattern you can build in their place? Name some tools, resources, or people that can support you.

Remind Me Again

When I forget who I am . . .
the stars in the sky remind me
just as the dark reminds me
the sand and soil remind me
just as the waves remind me
of the nature outside me
just as the nature inside me

Reminds me again
and again and again,
reminds me
again and again
Who I am
that I am
that I am
Yes, I am,
reminds me
who I am
yet again.

When I forget who I am . . .
sacred words
within books and breath
remind me
the soul and song
within heart and drum
remind me
the electric flow
just as the quiet stillness
reminds me
the joy reminds me
just as the pain reminds me
of a universe outside me
just as a universe inside me

Reminds me again
and again and again,
reminds me
again and again
Who I am
that I am
that I am
Yes, I am,
reminds me
who I am
yet again.

When I forget who I am . . .
there is a divine love letter
written in every leaf of grass
and every drop of rain
and every golden streak of sunlight dancing across the face of the earth
baptizing our bodies with a brilliance
so warm and familiar
may we remember
we are as ancient as we are holy
and this truth is lost to us only
when our memory can no longer hold
the weight of its glory

An Unearthing Practice

Nature–whether the rain forests of Jamaica, the prairie plains of North Dakota, or the community gardens of North Minneapolis–reminds me of our sacred humanity. This is a nod to my second collection of poems, *Remind Me Again: Poems and Practices for Remembering Who We Are.*

I'm deeply grateful for how I'm reminded of who I am and whose I am through the many relationships in my life. We belong to each other–not in a sense of possession, but as an expression of our deep connection.

Because of this deep connection, each of our relationships can offer reflections of what's happening inside of us.

Without judgment, respond to these questions with compassion and curiosity:
What do I feel my relationship with my body reflects about me?
What do I feel my relationship with my family or community reflects about me?
What do I feel my relationships with the people outside my community reflect about me?
What do I feel my relationship with nature reflects about me?
What do I feel my relationship with God, the divine, or a higher power reflects about me?

After reflecting, write a letter to your future self offering needed reminders. Consider postdating the letter and mailing it to yourself to be opened several months or a year from now. You can also use this practice to write and send letters to others who may be in need of reminders about themselves.

Sun Flowers

We are like sunflowers
always facing the Sun

standing as tall as we can
and when those around us fall
we wrap around them
and lift them up
to stand as tall as they can

many are inspired and amazed
by the warmth and light in our gaze

it's the way we were made
it's our superpower
to amplify everyone's power

when we choose to share light
and choose to grow love
wherever we go
the sun flowers.

An Unearthing Practice

When I was growing up, we passed a field of sunflowers
on the way to our church.

Sunflowers are famously known for how they move to
face the sun from sunrise to sunset. They can inspire us
to not only face the sun, but to know that the light also
lives in us.

We don't need to dim others' lights to shine, nor do we
need to let our own light dim for others to shine. We
shine brighter together.

How can we practice seeing the light within each other?

FLOURISH

Poems for cultivating abundance

Thunderous Abundance

There is a thunderous abundance
above us and under us
within us and beyond us
for us and because of us

Like the raindrop
before the storm erupts
they may say "poor us"
but we're porous
because more and more is poured in us
that pours from the pores of us
it stores up until it restores us
our source will always resource us

No matter what storms come for us
there's always more
and more erupts
the same wind roars in us
through the core of us

No matter if we've said or done enough
the sun comes up and shines above us
the earth still produces fruit up under us
our body still holds us and loves us

Abundance is not only possible,
abundance is inevitable

When we look for abundance,
we see abundance everywhere.
.

An Unearthing Practice

One of my most harrowing adventures while driving between parishes in Jamaica happened when my car was stranded in the middle of the jungle during a rainstorm. Surprisingly, I made friends with strangers who came to help me out of the generosity and kindness of their hearts. While that situation could have very well ended differently, this was yet another example of how people have often shown up throughout my life in unexpected times and places to help me along the way.

I've noticed that when I look for abundance, I see more abundance.

Spend the next 24 hours counting your blessings and looking for ways things could be working out for your highest good, even if you need to playfully imagine an unlikely best-case scenario.

Poet Tree

It grows in me,
like a poet tree,
with branches and leaves,
stanzas and seeds,
a seed is planted in me,
planted in faith and growing in grace,
i can feel it dancing in me,
waving its hands and its feet,
waiting for its chance to be free

kicking against the mama's belly as it's swelling,
the shell screams
in pain as it's fluctuating,
like a burst of inspiration,
the shell cracking,
like an egg hatching,
the husk is dispersed
and thus a miraculous birth occurs

the seedling emerges from the earth headfirst,
searching the firmament for purpose and self-worth,
with sunlight, water, and dirt,
the seedling needs this trinity
to fully flourish,
one day a full forest,
but for now
a poet tree.

An Unearthing Practice

My favorite trees are the tropical evergreens that
grow ackee fruit, the national fruit of Jamaica that
is medicinally, culturally, and culinarily significant
throughout the Caribbean and beyond. Ackee begin as
small black seeds but over time grow into trees with
delicious bright-red fruit–a reminder that much of life
takes patience to open and unfold its fullest potential.

If you were a plant, what plant would you be?
Describe the color, size, shape.

Where would you be planted?

How would you grow?

Why would you grow?

Reflect on areas of your life that are calling for the
grace and patience required for growth.

‹Bigger Than›

We are > bigger:
We are > bigger than what we imagine,
bigger than > what we can fathom
bigger than > what has happened
or could ever happen

Bigger than > anxiety, bigger than > depression
Bigger than > violence, bigger than > oppression
We are bigger than > any book written
or any word we ever spell,
bigger than > any poem, song, or story
could ever tell

Bigger than > we think,
bigger than > we feel,
bigger like the wind
is to the ship
is to the sail

Bigger than > any passage, pathway,
road, route,
track, or trail

Bigger like the tree
is to the seed
is to the shell.

Are we bigger than > religion, culture, class, and race?
Are we bigger than > any finite point
defined in time and space?
Are we bigger than > our questions, our fears, and our mistakes?
Is anything we could ever be,
that's bigger than < God's grace?

An Unearthing Practice

Traveling outside of my hometown, outside of the state that I live in, and even outside of the US have all been experiences that taught me how I'm a part of a much bigger world than I once thought.

As a practice to explore your "bigness," write or draw pictures in response to each question on separate sticky notes or notecards:

What are your biggest failures, embarrassments, or mistakes?

What are your biggest successes, achievements, and accomplishments?

How would you identify your race, gender, sexual orientation, ability/disability, nationality, ethnicity?

Fold each note as small as you can and place them inside a jar as a reminder that, while these are all significant dimensions, who you are is bigger than any of your experiences or identities.

Comeback

This season of life
is called the comeback

Where everything that was taken
is bound to come back.

We've been waiting like springtime
after winter hibernation,
this will be the generation of regeneration.

Like
the flower that grows through cracks in the pavement
Like
light painting streaks of color after the rain ends

Like
clothes for the naked
Like
the unhoused
no longer forced to lay in tents
or struggling to pay rent
but get to stay in
a safe place that was made for them

Like
debts forgiven,
prisoners uncaged,
no orphans and widows
but families reclaimed

No longer remaining jaded,
the comeback is so close,
we can feel it,
we can taste it.

As it's coming back to us,
we're coming back to it,
no need to chase it.

As it's running back to us,
we're running back to it,
no time is wasted.

When the wind hits us harder than a punching bag,
when the air gets cold and sharper than a thumbtack,
when we feel it's far too soon
for the sunset,
remember,
after a while,
it will all come back.

An Unearthing Practice

The first time I visited Jamaica without my family was during a time of deep loss in my life. Experiencing loss can feel devastating. Some losses won't come back, and it can be healing to allow ourselves to grieve.

Accompanying others in their grief and loss can also be a part of a healing process.

Grief circles can be any space where we gather with others to work through our emotions. This is one way to come back to ourselves.

What are some ways you can build communal support in these moments?

Reap

If we can't see the change that we wanna be,
can we be the change that we wanna see?
If we don't reap the fruits that we want and need,
can we plant the seeds that we wanna reap?

If we can be the change that we wanna see
and plant the seeds that we wanna reap,
when it comes time for harvest
we'll have a whole heap.

An Unearthing Practice

"Whole heap" means "a large amount" in Patios or Patwah, which is an English-based creole language with West African, Taino, and European influences spoken throughout the Jamaican diaspora.

The only way to have a whole heap of something is to build upon it from the ground up. "One one coco full basket," or gathering one coconut at a time will fill the basket, is another Patwah way of saying it.

Write a list of the personal qualities or characteristics you want more of in your life. What are things you can say or do to practice embodying those qualities or characteristics?

Garden of Gratitude

I don't want to give you flowers.
I want to grow you a garden.

When I can give you more life,
why give you something dead?

Instead of a bouquet of flowers,
how about a flower bed?

I want to water you
in the most authentic ways possible,
a display of ways to blossom through
the poetry I offer you

Not perfectly written or presented,
but purposefully with intention
until you feel it
and know I meant it

Not perfectly worded,
but perfectly honest

like tending to the soil
is staying true to a promise,
like reaping the ripened
is a commitment to a harvest

this covenant of abundance
will keep us from starving

I don't want to give you flowers.
I want to grow you a garden.

I want to shower you
with as much love as your heart can hold
and let it flow and overflow
until your petals unfold

I want to take your senses on adventures,
with fragrances and flavors
we can savor every layer
and still save some for later

I want to give you room to grow
in ways you've never bloomed before

space to behold and be held,
prioritize your health,
become your favorite self,
build generational wealth

I want to give you
affirmation, honor, and encouragement

Only all that is nourishing
and aids in your flourishing

I don't want to give you flowers.
I want to grow you a garden.

A garden planted for us,
a garden planted within us,
when we put our soul and heart in
it always replenishes.

It's that simple.
Everyone should know
how to plant something
and make it grow.
Let's plant our broken hearts
and watch them make us whole.

An Unearthing Practice

Planting pineapples and yams sparked dreams of being a part of a community garden or urban farm where people plant and grow different foods to share with each other as a sustainable ecovillage.

Growing our own food can be enlightening and empowering. We can learn so much from plants and each other.

Sit with some plants. Study them. Observe them. Listen to them. What stories are they telling you?

Whether it's a house plant, a plot in a community garden, or crops at a farm, find an opportunity to watch something as it grows, from seed to sprout to flower or fruit.

Reflect on how the relationships in your life go through a similar process of development. How can you practice gratitude in each stage you're in?

Explore creative ways to express your gratitude toward those with you in the process.

Many Rivers

I've known rivers
many rivers

From the Tigris, Euphrates, and the Nile
they have ancient ways of curving like a signature smile.

I've known rivers
many rivers

From the Mekong, the Indus, the Ganges, and Xijiang
they've made the world dance with songs they sang.

I've known rivers
many rivers

From the Hudson, Potomac, Mississippi, and the Rio Grande
they all give beauty in their own way.

Blue, green, and turquoise
so silent, so full of noise,
so violent, so full of poise,
the waves lament as they rejoice.

I've known rivers
many rivers

. . . all these ways of flowing
. . . all these ways of knowing
. . . back to the same ocean.

. . . and in all these ways of water
we walk each other back home again.

. . . all these ways of being,
. . . all these ways to become.

I've known many rivers,
and out of many,
One.

An Unearthing Practice

Every time I'm near a body of water–whether it's a waterfall, ocean, lake, or river–it has a calming, soothing effect on me. I love that our bodies and our planet are both made up of mostly water and can serve as reminders of how differences and similarities coexist harmoniously.

Notice all the things you have in common with people that you meet.

Notice all the things that differ between you and the people you meet.

How can conflict and tension give rise to new possibilities? How can you honor, affirm, and celebrate the similarities and the differences?

Acknowledgements

How can I even begin to express my immense gratitude to those who have so generously given of themselves?

Thank you to my family for being the first to show me what unconditional love means. We got that overflowing love!

Thank you to my mentors, teachers, and friends who have helped me unearth and reroot myself in ways I couldn't have done alone. No matter where I'm rooted, you'll always be a reason for my growth.

A special thank you to Dawn Rundman for being my biggest champion on this author journey. This book wouldn't exist without you.

Thank you to Jafud for reminding me of my purpose as an artist and healer and inviting me into deeper practice.

And to my village, all of you who practice alongside me:

I don't want to give you flowers.
I want to grow you a garden.

Jafud and Joe
Photo by Elliot Malcolm